AF504391

Cosmo's Deep Sea Adventure

By Kathryn Gomes

Dedicated to my students.

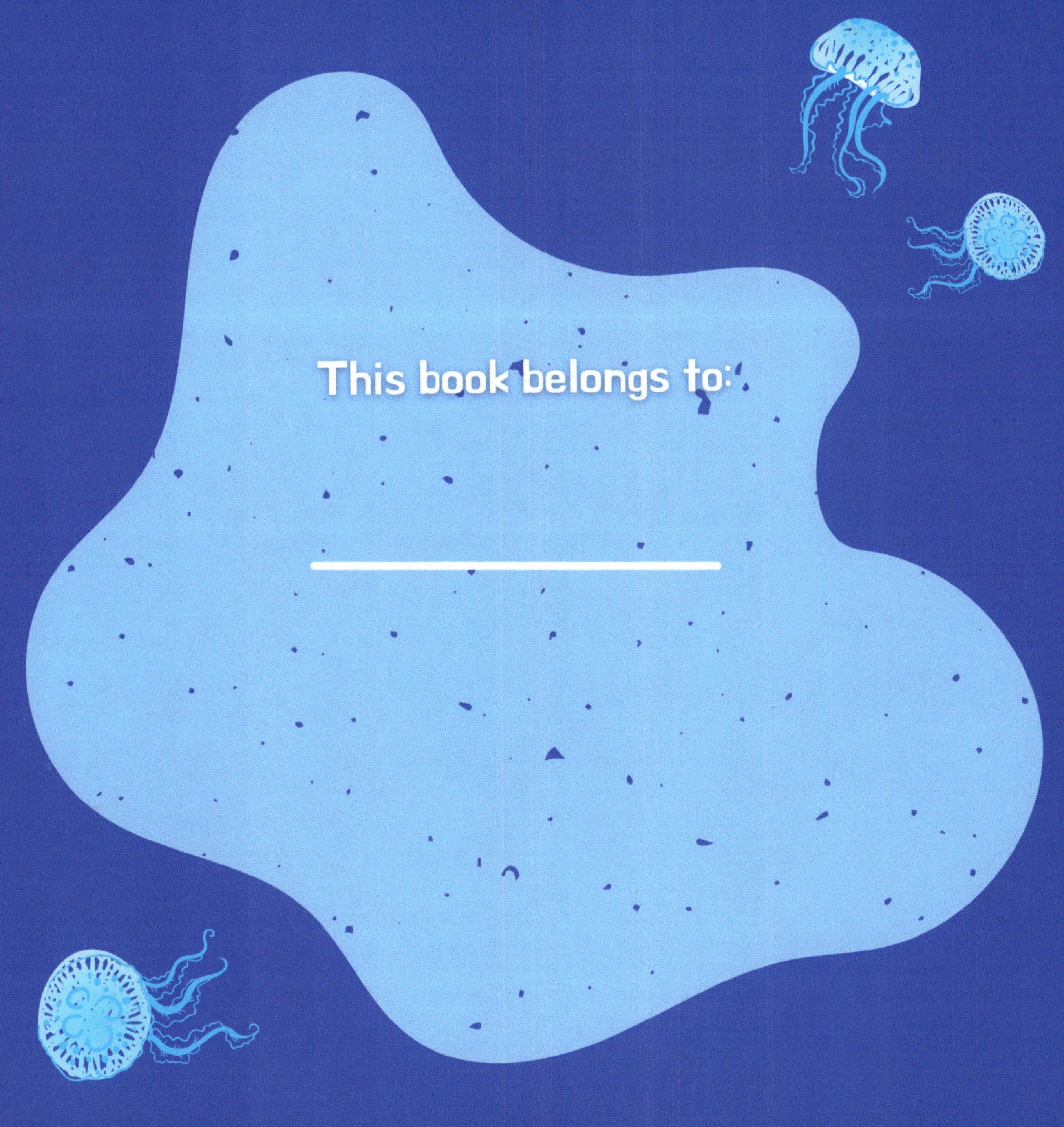
This book belongs to:

Hello there!

It's me again, Cosmo, and I am so excited to embark on another great adventure together. This time, I will take you to a place just as mysterious and exciting as outer space, the ocean! So slip on your diving gear and step onboard my latest, greatest submarine- "The Slippery Flipper." From the waves of the Sunlight Zone to the dark and mysterious trenches of the Abyssal zone, I'll show you all of the wonders that our oceans have to offer.

Come on then, let's dive into this underwater adveture together!

Our first stop is the Sunlight Zone. Isn't it beautiful down here? So clear and bright. There's lots of sea life to be found here, such as jelly fish, sea turtles, colorful fish, sharks, dolphins, and stingrays. This is also where penguins like me prefer to swim!

Did you know?

The Sunlight zone is where almost all ocean plants live because they need sunlight to grow.

Welcome to the Twilight Zone. It is between 200 and 1,000 meters below the ocean surface, far too deep for a scuba diver to swim. The weight of the water creates a huge amount of pressure. Quick! Let's get back to the Slippery Flipper so we can safely continue our decent down into the ocean depths!

Did you know?

The twilight zone is home to more fish than the rest of the ocean combined.

Time to look out the porthole window, everyone! See that tall, dark mountain ahead? That's a volcano sitting right on the ocean floor. Can you spot the bubbles rising up from it? Those are actually gases escaping from within the volcano! These underwater giants erupt just like volcanoes on land do! They spew hot lava into the water, which eventually turn into Islands.

Did you know?

The hydrothermal vent, where hot water gushes out of an underwater volcano, makes a cozy home for some incredible sea creatures!

We are now arriving at the third layer of the ocean. This is known as the Midnight Zone. It is between 1,000 to 4,000 meters deep. It sure is dark down here! There is no natural light and the water is REALLY cold. This zone is home to some very strange-looking creatures! Some even create their own light, using something called bioluminescence.

Did you know?

The depth at which the famous ship called Titanic Sank is 3,800 m deep in the Midnight Zone.

Finally, we are here on the ocean basin- known as the Abyssal Zone. We are currently located approximately 4,000 - 6,000 meters below the surface of the ocean. Only very specialized submersibles can reach these extreme depths. Good thing The Slippery Flipper is one of them! Strap on your night-vision goggles because it is completely dark down here. Sea spiders, the fang-tooth fish, and colossal squid are just some of the unique and puzzling creatures that visit this abyss.

Did you know?

The deepest known part of the ocean is called the Mariana Trench.

Well, explorers, our tour must end here. It's not safe to travel any deeper. Time to ascend back up to the surface and get the Slippery Flipper back to some sunlight. This might take awhile, so while we wait, let's discuss a few more fun facts about ocean exploration...

Strange Creatures of the Sea

We met some pretty wild sea creatures along this journey, and the ocean is full of even weirder ones! Take the Hawaiian bobtail squid, for example, which has the ability to glow in the dark! But it's not glowing like a flashlight. Instead, it has a bunch of tiny glowing bacteria that live inside of its body!

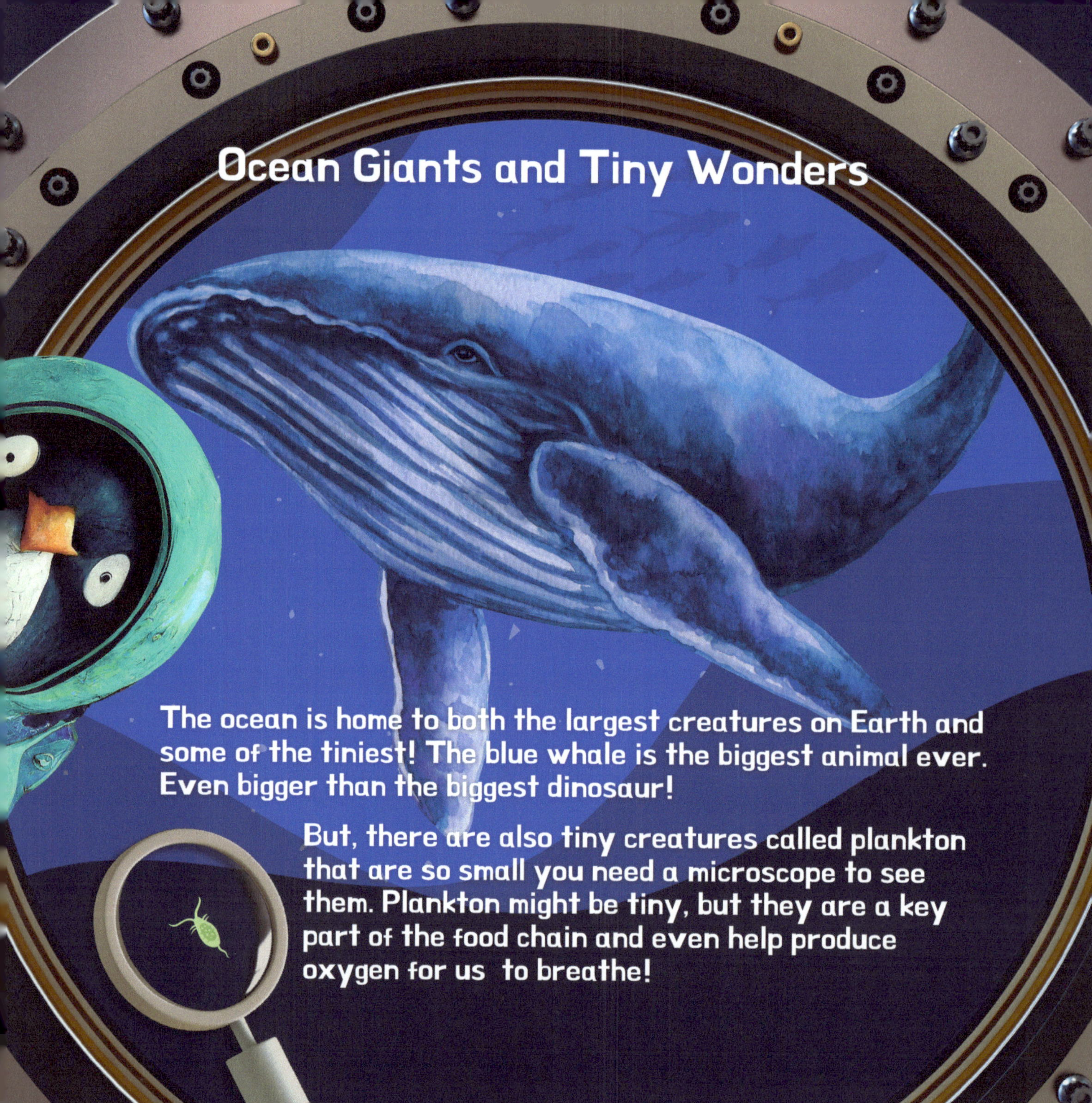

Ocean Giants and Tiny Wonders

The ocean is home to both the largest creatures on Earth and some of the tiniest! The blue whale is the biggest animal ever. Even bigger than the biggest dinosaur!

But, there are also tiny creatures called plankton that are so small you need a microscope to see them. Plankton might be tiny, but they are a key part of the food chain and even help produce oxygen for us to breathe!

The Deep-Sea Pioneers

Many explorers just like us have taken some incredible journeys to the bottom of the ocean! In 1960, the U.S. Navy used a submersible called the Trieste to take two brave explorers to the Mariana Trench for the very first time. That's over 10,000 meters deep! In 2012, a filmmaker named James Cameron made the same journey in a submersible called the Deepsea Challenger. What an adventure!

The Evolution of Diving Suits

Diving deep into the ocean wasn't always easy or as stylish, like my diving suit! The first diving suits were big and bulky—made of very heavy metal, and had long hoses connecting them to the surface. But over time, diving suits improved. Now, divers can wear sleek, lightweight suits that let them explore the deep sea more easily.

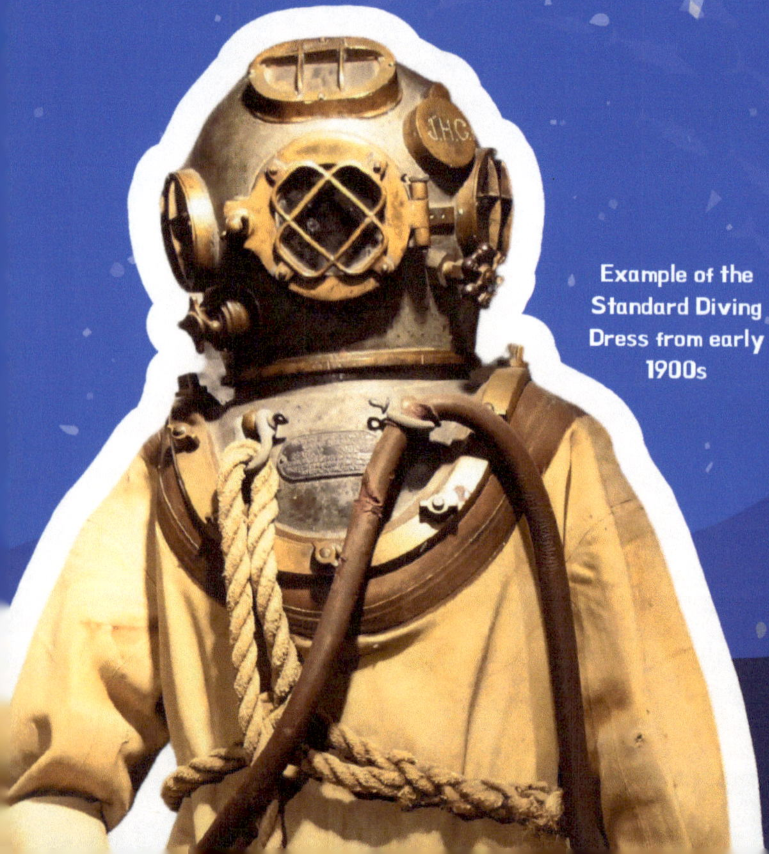

Example of the Standard Diving Dress from early 1900s

Ocean Robots

Some parts of the ocean are so deep and dark that humans can't explore them on their own. That's where our awesome robot friends come in! These ocean robots, also known as ROVs, have helped scientists to discover all kinds of new species of animals, underwater volcanoes, and even shipwrecks lost for hundreds of years! Isn't that amazing?

Protecting Our Blue Planet

Today we discovered so many amazing things about the ocean, but perhaps you also noticed some problems. Plastic and trash in the water can hurt sea animals. Pollution makes it hard for them to live. But there's hope! People around the world are working hard to clean up the ocean and protect sea life, and so can you! Even small actions, like reducing plastic use, recycling, and keeping beaches clean, can make a big difference!

The Mystery of the Deep

Together we have explored every level of the ocean, but there's still so much we don't know. Scientists believe that more than 80% of the ocean remains unexplored! Some areas are so deep that even the best underwater robots can't reach them, yet. Perhaps someday, we will return together to discover more hidden secrets of the sea!

Here we are back at the surface!
Great job, explorers! What a ride!
But this journey has made me quite hungry.
Raise a flipper if you'd like to share a sardine sandwich?

Until next time- this is your captain, Cosmo. Time for lunch...

Glossary

Abyss: The deepest part of the ocean, where it's very dark, cold, and mysterious.

Bioluminescence: The ability of some sea creatures to produce light, making them glow in the dark, deep ocean.

Deep-Sea Submarine: A special underwater vehicle that can dive very deep into the ocean, where regular submarines cannot go.

Exploration: The act of traveling through unknown areas to learn and discover new things, like scientists exploring the deep ocean.

Hydrothermal Vent: A hydrothermal vent is like a big underwater chimney that blows out super hot water from inside the Earth. It's found deep in the ocean.

Midnight Zone: A dark, cold layer of the ocean where sunlight doesn't reach, and many creatures use bioluminescence.

Plankton: Tiny sea creatures and plants that float in the water and are very important as food for many sea animals.

Microscope: A tool that helps you see really tiny things, like germs or the details of a leaf, up close.

Pressure: The force you feel when something pushes you. For example, the water pressing down as you go deeper in the ocean. The deeper you go, the stronger the pressure gets.

ROV (Remotely Operated Vehicle): A robot controlled by scientists from a ship, used to explore deep parts of the ocean where it's too dangerous for humans to go.

Sunlight zone: The top layer of the ocean where sunlight can reach. It's warm, bright, and where most sea animals, like fish and dolphins, live.

Titanic: The Titanic was a huge ship that sank a long time ago after hitting an iceberg. It's now sitting at the bottom of the ocean, and people are still fascinated by its story today.

Trench: A very deep, narrow canyon in the ocean floor, often the deepest parts of the ocean.

Underwater Volcano: An underwater volcano is like a mountain under the sea that sometimes bursts and spills out melted rock called lava. It makes the ocean floor grow!

About the Author

Kathryn Gomes is an elementary school teacher with a Masters of Science in Education. Living near Florida's beautiful beaches, Kathryn was inspired to make Cosmo's next big adventure dive deep into the ocean!